ROTHERHAM
PAST & PRESENT

Hunter's Tea Stores, 39 High Street, 1911. This window won first prize in the Rotherham Shopping Week. (*Rotherham Archives & Local Studies 17846*)

ROTHERHAM
PAST & PRESENT

ANTHONY MUNFORD

First published in the United Kingdom in 2001 by Sutton Publishing Limited

This new paperback edition first published in 2010 by The History Press
The History Press
The Mill, Brimscombe Port,
Stroud, Gloucestershire, GL5 2QG
www.thehistorypress.co.uk

British Library Cataloguing in Publication Data
A catalogue record for this book is available from the British Library.

ISBN 978-0-7524-5769-7

Illustrations

Front endpaper: Rotherham from the church tower, 1926. During the long coal strike of 1926, while there was no smoke from coal fires to obscure the view, an anonymous photographer took a series of photographs from the church tower. In the foreground is the mock-Tudor Grapes Inn on College Street. At mid-left are the parish church schools on College Lane with the Regent Theatre beyond. The spire at the left is that of St Stephen's Church on St Ann's Road, while the spire at top right is that of the Congregational Church on Doncaster Gate. (*Rotherham Archives & Local Studies 0071*)

Back endpaper: Looking north from the parish church, 1926. The Municipal Offices on Howard Street can be seen at the right with the waterworks pumping station on Frederick Street and the gasworks beyond. In the distance, to the right of the waterworks' chimney, is the power station on Rawmarsh Road. Bridgegate is at bottom left. (*Rotherham Archives & Local Studies 097*)

Half-title page: Bridgegate from the church tower, 1928. Bridgegate is in the last stages of widening and work has started on demolishing the buildings on the corner with Millgate. (*Rotherham Archives & Local Studies 8709*)

Title page: Talbot Lane Methodist Church, viewed across the Cattle Market, *c.* 1905. This church replaced its nineteenth-century predecessor, which was destroyed by fire in 1901. (*Rotherham Archives & Local Studies 2537*)

Typesetting and origination by
Sutton Publishing Limited.
Printed and bound in England

Contents

INTRODUCTION   11

CHURCH STREET, CORPORATION STREET &
    HIGH STREET   17

COLLEGE STREET, BRIDGEGATE & HOWARD STREET   37

WELLGATE & WESTGATE   57

EFFINGHAM STREET & FREDERICK STREET   81

MOORGATE STREET & MOORGATE ROAD   95

DONCASTER GATE & DONCASTER ROAD   105

MASBROUGH & KIMBERWORTH   113

SUBURBIA   121

ACKNOWLEDGEMENTS   125

John Mason, watchmaker and jeweller, *c*. 1880. John Mason had shops in Doncaster Gate and College Street before settling at 16 High Street in the 1860s. He moved to the present shop, 36 High Street, in about 1880. In 1910 the Yorkshire Penny Bank occupied this building. (*Rotherham Archives & Local Studies 14226*)

Introduction

At the opening of the twentieth century Rotherham was a town of some 54,000 people, firmly established as an internationally renowned centre of the iron and steel industry. It had not always been so. Medieval Rotherham was an important market town, based on its control of an important crossing-point of the River Don, and the centre of a parish encompassing the townships of Rotherham, Kimberworth, Greasbrough, Tinsley, Brinsworth, Catcliffe and Orgreave. By the end of the fifteenth century, however, Rotherham was the envy of the other towns in the area, with its splendid Perpendicular-style parish church, its Chapel on the Bridge and its College of Jesus.

The Romans had exploited the iron ores in the area, and more effective mining and smelting was begun at Kimberworth in the twelfth century. The sixteenth and seventeenth centuries saw increased industrialisation with the establishment of a blast furnace and slitting mill at Masbrough. Major industrial development followed in the mid-eighteenth century when the opening of the Don Navigation to Rotherham in 1740 persuaded the Walker brothers to move their iron-founding business from Grenoside to Masbrough. By the end of the century the Walkers' works were among the largest in the country, producing everything from cooking pots to naval cannon and iron bridges. In the nineteenth century other industrialists built on the foundations laid by the Walkers and Rotherham became a national centre for the steel, iron, glass-making and brass-casting industries.

The nineteenth century brought widespread changes to the town. Industry was mainly confined to the Masbrough side of the Don. Housing for the workers sprang up both in that area and within the town centre. Property developers crammed courts of poor-quality housing on to every available plot of land. The population, which had been 7,500 in 1801, had risen to 15,000 by 1851. Of these 6,000 lived in the township of Rotherham and 9,000 in Kimberworth and Masbrough.

With the exception of the Feoffees of the Common Lands and the Lighting Commissioners (established in 1801), there was no formal local government. The growth had taken place without any planning and without the provision of sewers and drains. The main water supply remained private wells and the springs in Wellgate. These facts contributed to the outbreak of cholera in 1832. Matters came to head in 1851 when, as the result of a local petition, a government inspector heard a litany of evidence of cellars flooded with foul water (and worse) and wells contaminated from cesspits. This enquiry resulted in the establishment of an elected Board of Health for Rotherham and Kimberworth. The new Board set to work to improve the town, establishing a proper piped water supply, constructing sewers and drains and taking over the private gasworks.

Until the 1850s the town centre looked much as it had done in the Middle Ages with the parish church and Market Place in the centre surrounded by the main streets – High Street, College Street (formerly Jesus Gate and before that Brook Gate) and Church Street (or Ratten Row), from which radiated Bridgegate, Doncaster Gate, Wellgate and Westgate. The lords of the manor, the Earls of Effingham, owned the land to the north of College Street and Bridgegate but were unable to develop the area because a family settlement restricted them to leases of only twenty-one years. In 1850 the current earl obtained a private Act of Parliament breaking the entail and was then able to lay out a network of new streets (Howard Street, Effingham Street, Frederick Street, etc.) and to begin leasing plots. Among his first customers was the Local Board who erected offices on Howard Street, the embryonic town hall. The town began to expand northwards, aided by the Badger family, solicitors and property developers, who purchased the Eastwood Estate and laid it out for building.

In the mid-nineteenth century the education available to the population at large was limited to the Grammar School (a survivor from the College of Jesus), the National Schools run by the parish church, the Feoffees' charity school, the nonconformist British School

A modern version of the view on the front endpaper, 2001. The Grapes Inn is now Marks & Spencer, with Rotherham College Art and Technology behind. The Regent has been replaced by the Centenary Market and the spire of St Stephen's Church is visible on the skyline. (*Author*)

)king south from the church tower, 1926. The Church of Our Father on Moorgate Street can be seen at top right. In the ∍eground are the backs of the shops on the High Street. The barn-like structure at the left is the Whitehall Cinema and just ɔve it are the tower and dome of the Primitive Methodist Chapel, Wellgate. (*Rotherham Archives & Local Studies 070*)

and Hollis School, and a number of small private schools. The majority of children in the town had no opportunity for education. This changed in 1875 with the establishment of the Rotherham School Board which began to build Board schools in all areas of the town. In 1871 the town successfully petitioned the Crown to be created a borough with a mayor and corporation. A market hall was erected in the Market Place in 1879, but it had to be completely rebuilt in 1889 after being destroyed by fire. In 1902 the town was granted county borough status and in 1903 the council took over the responsibilities of the School Board.

The year 1903 also saw the running of the first trams. Powers to establish a network of tram services had been obtained in 1900 and the necessary power station, on Rawmarsh Road, had been opened in 1901. The new tram system necessitated a number of improvements in the town, including the building of Coronation Bridge at Masbrough, the construction of Corporation Street, linking the Market Place with Rotherham Bridge,

Looking south from the church tower, 2001. The Church of Our Father, now a mosque, is still visible above the roof of the to hall. The Whitehall Cinema has been replaced with Primark (formerly British Home Stores) and the Primitive Methodist Cha is now the Masonic Hall. (*Author*)

and the widening of the top of High Street. The latter involved the demolition of the early nineteenth-century Shambles, subsequently replaced with Imperial Buildings.

Rotherham's contribution to the First World War is evidenced by the 1,304 names inscribed on the cenotaph in Clifton Park (unveiled in 1922) and the war effort of the local industries. The construction of a ¼-mile-long melting shop at Steel, Peech & Tozer, to meet the wartime demand for steel, resulted in the excavation of the Roman fort at Templebrough, which lay beneath the site. Immediately after the war ended, the borough council was able to start tackling the problem of the large numbers of slum houses in the town. Armed with new powers from the government, the council purchased an estate at East Dene and began to build council houses for rent. Once there was a sufficient stock of houses, the council embarked on an ambitious slum clearance campaign, demolishing the courts of slum houses that lay behind the town centre streets and at Masbrough. By 1939 Rotherham Borough Council had constructed houses at twice the national rate. Almost 1,200 unfit houses had been demolished and nearly 5,000 new houses erected. The growth of council housing was paralleled by the growth of private housing, with numbers of suburban semi-detached houses being built on the outskirts of the town.

The Chapel on the Bridge had led a chequered existence since its suppression in 1547, serving variously as almshouses, the town jail and a tobacconist's shop. The shop owner was bought out in 1913 and after restoration the chapel was reconsecrated in 1924. By this time the medieval bridge was beginning to show its age so the council constructed the new Chantry Bridge alongside in 1930. A major change in the town centre was the widening of Bridgegate to allow buses and trolley-buses access to the new All Saints Square, opened in 1933. A new Court House was opened in the Crofts in 1929, replacing the nineteenth-century building on Effingham Street.

Rotherham did not avoid the problems caused by the great depression of the 1920s and in 1930 there were 15,000 unemployed in the town. Meadow Bank Road was constructed to provide work and other road-building schemes also helped to alleviate the problem. Herringthorpe Valley Road, opened in 1933 as a joint venture with the West Riding County Council, was part of a proposed ring road. The narrow Castle Sike Lane from Whiston crossroads to the Brecks was converted into a dual carriageway, called East Bawtry Road, in 1937. A year earlier the boundaries of the borough had been extended to take in Greasbrough and parts of Whiston, Brinsworth and Dalton.

The council embarked on other house-building programmes, at East Herringthorpe and Broom Valley, after the Second World War. The last tram ran in 1949 but the trolley-

king north from the church tower, July 2001. For a 1926 view, see the rear endpaper. (*Author*)

buses remained until 1965. The buses moved to the new bus station in 1971, allowing All Saints Square to be pedestrianised. Major changes to the town's geography came in the late 1960s with the clearance of large areas of Victorian housing between Effingham Square and St Ann's Road. Part of the cleared area was used to construct new council office blocks (Crinoline House, Civic Building and Norfolk House). Other clearances were to make way for Centenary Way, the new inner ring road to the M1, begun in 1969 and completed in 1995. Much property at Masbrough was also demolished to make way for the new road. In 1967 the Rotherham Police (founded in 1882) amalgamated with the Sheffield Police, the unified force becoming part of South Yorkshire Police in 1974.

In 1971 the borough council celebrated its centenary. The borough's population was then 85,000. Also in that year the markets were moved from the medieval Market Place to the new Centenary Markets off Howard Street. Three years later the county borough council was replaced by a new local authority. Rotherham became the centre of the Metropolitan Borough of Rotherham, with an area of 69,000 acres and a population of 243,000. The town hall on Howard Street became too small for the enlarged council, which moved into temporary accommodation across the road in the Transport Buildings. The old town hall was sold for conversion into a shopping arcade. In 1995 the former West Riding Court House on the Crofts, redundant once the new Court House at the Statutes was opened, was converted into a new town hall. With the majority of the through traffic diverted along Centenary Way, the council was able to pedestrianise most of the town centre streets in the 1980s and 1990s. In general, the 1980s were a difficult time for Rotherham with the run-down of the traditional steel and mining industries and the town centre suffering from competition from out-of-town shopping centres. The 1990s, however, saw signs of revival, both in the industrial and the retail sectors.

A time traveller from 1900 would find little to recognise in Rotherham today apart from the parish church and the Chapel on the Bridge. The photographs in this book have been carefully chosen to illustrate some of the changes that the town has undergone over the past century.

Church Street, Corporation Street & High Street

All Saints' parish church, *c.* 1870. The sundial on the porch of Rotherham parish church was removed during the restoration carried out by Gilbert Scott in 1873–5, dating this photograph to about 1870. The Norman font, visible outside the south transept, was moved inside as part of the restoration. (*Rotherham Archives & Local Studies 1740*)

All Saints' parish church, 2001. Here the view of the church is blocked by the weeping ash in the centre of the churchyard. The churchyard was closed to new burials in 1854 and most of the gravestones were removed in 1950. The lamp standards in the churchyard are replicas of the gas lamps that used to light the town. (*Author*)

Market Street, 1971. The last days of Rotherham's medieval Market Place in 1971 just before the move to the Centenary Market. The Market Hall of 1889 is at the right with the National Provincial Bank, originally the Sheffield Banking Co., on the left. (*Rotherham Archives & Local Studies 2988*)

Market Street, 2001. The Market Hall was demolished soon after the move to the Centenary Market and a car park now occupies the site. The National Provincial Bank is now the NatWest. (*Author*)

H. Taylor's shop in the Shambles, *c.* 1900. It would be a modern environmental health officer's nightmare! George H. Tay claimed to have been the rabbit king 'since before the Flood' but most of the produce arrayed on his stall in the Sham consists of poultry and game birds. The stone-built Shambles had been constructed in 1804 to replace the previous huddl butchers' and fishmongers' stalls. (*Rotherham Archives & Local Studies 2970*)

Centenary Market, 200
This is the indoor sectio
which is open Monday
to Saturday. There is an
outdoor general market
on Monday, Friday and
Saturday, with second-
hand clothes on Tuesda
and antiques and bric-
a-brac on Wednesday.
(*Author*)

Corporation Street, July 1936. This street was constructed in 1913 to connect the Market Place with Rotherham Bridge. This view shows the start of demolition of the block between Market Street and Millgate. The posters on the hoardings advertise Ginger Rogers and Fred Astaire in 'Top Hat' at the Premier, and Bette Davis and George Brent in 'Special Agent' at the Hippodrome. The Market Hall is visible at the top of the hill. (*Rotherham Archives & Local Studies 2193*)

Corporation Street, 2001. The hoardings have been replaced by All Saints Buildings. Construction of this block stopped at the outbreak of the Second World War and it was not finished until the mid-1950s. (*Author*)

The Empire Theatre and its associated shops and offices, *c.* 1915. The Empire was constructed on the site of the Cross Daggers inn, at the junction of Ship Hill and the High Street and opened in 1913. Moving pictures were part of the entertainment from the start but in 1921 it was converted wholly to a cinema. (*Rotherham Archives & Local Studies 15869*)

The Classic Cinema (formerly Empire), 14 April 1978. The Empire retained that name until 1955 when it became the Essoldo. In 1972 it was renamed the Classic and for the last two years of its life it was the Cannon. (*Rotherham Archives & Local Studies 2389*)

The former Empire, July 2001. Closure in 1990 was followed by a long period of disuse until the interior was converted into a complex of bars known as New York, New York. The main entrance on the High Street remains unused. (*Author*)

e High Street, *c.* 1890. The
part of the High Street was so
rrow that it was known as the
ttleneck'. This became awkward
1903 when the corporation
gan running trams up the High
eet. The property shown here,
th Robert Laycock's chemist's
p on the corner, and the
ambles, just visible behind it,
re demolished and replaced
h Imperial Buildings, opened in
08. (*Rotherham Archives & Local
dies 2316*)

erial Buildings, seen here in the early 1920s, still present much the same appearance today. A few years ago the borough
icil replaced the shop windows with replicas of the Edwardian originals. (*Rotherham Archives & Local Studies 8885*)

The Crown Hotel site, July 2001. The Crown survived until 1968. Cane World, with a Yorkshire Bank branch over, now occupies the site. In the background is the former Rotherham Co-operative Society building on Westgate. (*Author*)

The Crown Hotel, High Street, *c.* 1895. The largest inn in the town centre, the Crown was rebuilt in this form after Moorgate Street was cut through to the Crofts in about 1880, reducing the hotel to half its former frontage. (*Rotherham Archives & Local Studies 2396*)

The High Street, looking east, *c.* 1920. The shops on the left-hand side of the High Street included Percy Davy, chemist; William Blackburn & Co. Ltd, clothiers; John Fawcett Ltd, grocer; the Maypole Dairy; and, at nos 22,

23, 25 and 26, J.W. Muntus, drapers and silk mercers. (*Rotherham Archives & Local Studies 10022*)

The High Street, looking east, 1984. Little has changed in the basic structure of the shops since the 1920s, although the bay window has gone from no. 26. Nos 22–30 were amalgamated into Muntus's department store, which closed in 1988. (*Rotherham Archives & Local Studies 2342*)

The High Street, July 2001. The High Street was pedestrianised in 1993. The former Muntus's store was converted into a public house, one of the Old Monk chain, in the late 1990s. (*Author*)

High Street, south side, 1984. The timber-framed former Three Cranes (centre), the oldest secular building in the town
[cen]tre, was for many years occupied by Wakefield's Army Stores. It was originally twice the size but Freeman, Hardy & Willis
[dem]olished the lower half to make way for their modern shop in the 1960s. Wakefield's shop extended into 29 High Street, an
[eigh]teenth-century building that was the home of the Badger family, solicitors, for much of the nineteenth century. (*Rotherham*
[Arch]ives & Local Studies 2344)

High Street, south side,
2001. Today the Three
[Cran]es stands forlorn, having
[been] waiting for a new use
[since] Wakefield's moved out
[in th]e 1980s. Freeman, Hardy
[& Wi]llis's shop has become
[a Chi]nese restaurant, while
[Marc]h the Tailor's is an Italian
[resta]urant. (*Author*)

John H. Humphrey, pawnbroker, jeweller, clothier and outfitter, High Street, c. 1910. 'murder mystery near Barnsley' on the news placard has so far defi identification. The ent the left gave access to alleyway known as Sn Hill (originally Snell's leading up to the Crof (*Rotherham Archives & Local Studies 1173*)

The Rotherham Chamber Tec shop now stands where Humphrey's stood. The entry beneath the 'RCT' sign still gives acce Snail Hill. (*Author*)

h Bros, Rotherham, Ltd,
mongers, 14 High Street,
5. The windows are
ially decorated for George
ubilee. One is devoted to
age, one to gas lights,
to pots and pans and
ourth to tennis rackets.
herham Archives & Local
es 14727)

former Smith Bros' shop,
2001. The Careers Centre
pies the surviving portion
e original shop, the upper
having been demolished
rebuilt. (*Author*)

The Old Bank, High Street, 1892. The Old Bank was in fact the seventeenth-century town house of the Mountenoy family. It is thought that this is the house in which Charles I spent a night in 1647 and that Mary, Queen of Scots, was lodged in an earlier house on this site in 1569. Founded as a private bank by Walkers, Eyre & Stanley in 1792, it later became a branch of the Sheffield & Rotherham Bank which was absorbed by William's & Glyn's. (*Rotherham Archives & Local Studies 2311*)

Old Bank Buildings, High Street, July 2001. The Old Bank was demolished, along with the property on either side, in 1892 when the present bank, now the Royal Bank of Scotland, was erected. (*Author*)

Street, north side, *c.* 1910. Scales & Sons' boot and shoe warehouse stood on the corner of High Street and College Street, J.J. Cox, tailor, to its left. Then came the Elephant and Castle, Langton & Sons, boot manufacturers, and Boots the Chemists its blind out). (*Rotherham Archives & Local Studies 452*)

Street, north side, July . Scales & Sons, which d in 1926, and the ant and Castle were lished in 1932 when on's new building was ed. The Elephant and e's licence was transferred Park Hotel on Badsley Lane. (*Author*)

35

The High Street from Doncaster Gate, *c.* 1895. The clock on Scales & Sons and the shadows indicate that this photograph was taken at 7.05 a.m., hence the lack of traffic. The three-storey building on the corner of College Road was the King's Arms. The photographer is standing outside the Wheatsheaf and the Pack Horse Inn stands on the corner of Wellgate. (*Rotherham Archives & Local Studies 2313*)

The High Street from Doncaster Gate, July 2001. The Pack Horse closed in 1904, to be replaced with a block of shops. The King's Arms made way for W.H. Smith's in 1966 while the Wheatsheaf lasted until 1968. (*Author*)

College Street, Bridgegate & Howard Street

College Street, 2001. A typical Burton's shop replaced Scales & Sons in the 1930s. Burton's had previously had a shop on the High Street. Woolworth's now stands where the College Inn once was. (*Author*)

College Street, *c.* 1905. Named after the College of Jesus, constructed in 1485, this street was formerly known as Brookgate. The College Inn can be seen in the centre distance. The King's Arms stands on the right with Scales & Sons' premises to the left. (*Rotherham Archives & Local Studies 10971*)

Henry Gough's shop, 36a College Street, *c.* 1920. Gough had several grocery shops in the town. This one stood at the corner of Vicarage Lane and was photographed during a promotion for Golden Fleece margarine. Gough's other shops were on High Street, Westgate, Frederick Street and Broad Street, Parkgate. (*Rotherham Archives & Local Studies 15286*)

No. 36a College Street, July 2001. R.H. Gilling redeveloped the block that contained Gough's shop in 1931–2, to designs by James Totty. The site of Gough's grocery is now occupied by Specsavers. (*Author*)

College Inn and Court House, *c.* 1895. The College Inn was one wing of the fifteenth-century College of Jesus, founded by ᴍas Rotherham, Archbishop of York, in 1485 and suppressed in 1547. At left is the Court House of 1826, and above the ᴏf Dismore's Oyster Saloon can be seen the roofs of the parish church schools on College Lane. (*Rotherham Archives & Local ʟies 2170*)

ᴏ corner of College
ᴇt and Effingham
ᴇt, July 2001. Much
ᴉeval brickwork
ᴀ the College Inn
incorporated in
ᴏew College Inn
ᴇffingham Street
ᴉ Woolworth's
ᴠeloped the corner
ᴉ 1930. The Court
ᴋe closed in 1929
ᴉ the new Court
ᴋe in the Crofts
ᴇd. (*Author*)

College Square, *c.* 1900. This elaborate gas lamp stood in front of the Court House in College Square, replacing the single seen on the previous page. The building occupied by the Sheffield & Hallamshire Bank (later Barclays) was erected in 182 the Rotherham Dispensary, which closed when Doncaster Gate Hospital opened in 1872. (*Rotherham Archives & Local St 13617*)

All Saints Square from Effingham Street, July 2001. The old dispensa building was demolishe when All Saints Square constructed in 1933. T Borough Boot Co. gave to Davy's Tudor Café, n Radio Rentals, erected 1925 and modified in 1 (*Author*)

All Saints Square, 1935. Opened in 1933, All Saints Square was created by demolishing the property between the churchyard and College Street. This view shows the new Woolworth's building in the distance with the equally new College of Arts and Technology of 1931 behind it. A Rotherham Corporation trolley-bus is loading at the right with a Mexborough & Swinton Traction Co. trolley-bus in the centre. (*Rotherham Archives & Local Studies 11607*)

All Saints Square, July 2001. The square was pedestrianised in 1971 when the buses moved to the new bus station. It is currently in the final stages of remodelling. (*Author*)

Bridgegate, 1903. This view of Bridgegate at the turn of the twentieth century shows how narrow the street was until the corporation embarked on a widening scheme after the First World War to allow buses and trolley-buses access to the planned All Saints Square. The west side was demolished and rebuilt to a new alignment. The original Angel Inn is at the right, with Turner's pawnbroker's shop to its left. (*Rotherham Archives & Local Studies 10969*)

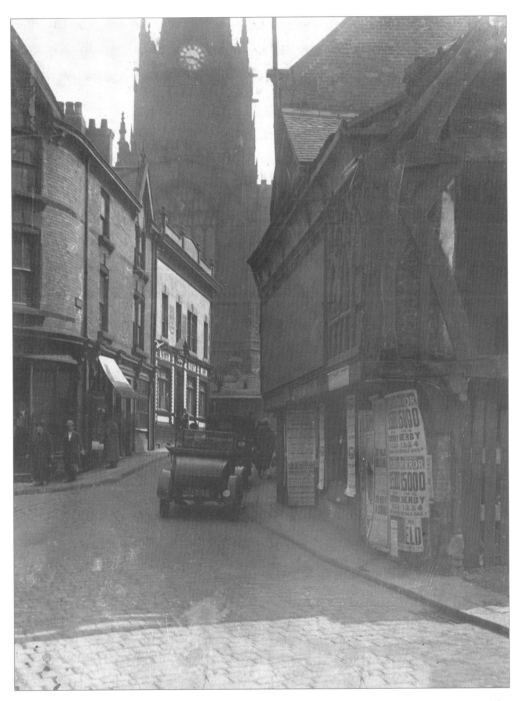

Bridgegate during widening, 1926. The late medieval Turf Tavern was demolished during the last stages of the expansion of Bridgegate. The massive timbers from which this old inn was constructed can just be made out in this view. The white building beyond the car was the White Hart, which closed in 1929. (*Rotherham Archives & Local Studies 01169*)

Bridgegate, July 2001. The street is now three times as wide as it used to be. The new Angel, of 1915, is at the right v̶ Turner's new shop (1925), now Alexon, next door. (*Author*)

Bridgegate, July 2001. The widening of Bridgegate and th₁ construction of All Saints Square openeᵈ up new vistas on thᵉ north side of the par₁ church. (*Author*)

Bridgegate from College Street, 1928. This shows the new property on the west side of Bridgegate, with John Law's draper's shop and Fawley's ironmonger's prominent. The blind outside Levy Bros' boot and shoe shop proclaims it to be the 'Original Boot Co.'. The site of the Turf Tavern (left) has not yet been paved. (*Rotherham Archives & Local Studies 01144*)

Bridgegate from College Street, July 2001. The shops of John Law and Fawley still exist under other names, but Levy's, latterly part of Peck's shop, gave way to a new McDonald's in the 1980s. At the extreme right can be seen the archway leading to the Red Lion. (*Author*)

The east side of Bridgegate, 1967. The mock-Tudor building, occupied by Blyth Model Dairies and Stuart's fashions, dates only from about 1930. The left-hand half of Hastings' furniture stores originated as the eighteenth-century town house of the Buck family. The lower building, to the left of Hastings, is Russum's, brush makers. (*Rotherham Archives & Local Studies 01112*)

The Buck house still exists, behind the tree, as a furniture shop, while the other half of Hastings' shop is now the Rhinoceros pub. J. and W. Hastings moved their business to Wickersley in 1982 and ceased trading in 1994. (*Author*)

...dgegate, *c.* 1975. Sheffield Furniture Co. occupies the corner, followed by Lee of Leeds (Bridgegate) Ltd, hairdressers' ...drymen; Lockwood's, florist; Bricknell's, newsagents and stationers; Davy's, chemist and druggist; the Café and Salon ...ene, ladies' hairdressers. (*Rotherham Archives & Local Studies 01128*)

...gegate, 2001. The shops ...e previous photograph ...e demolished as part of ...Cascades development ...983–4. The block is now ...pied by the Yorkshire ..., Going Places travel ...ts and the post office. ...hor)

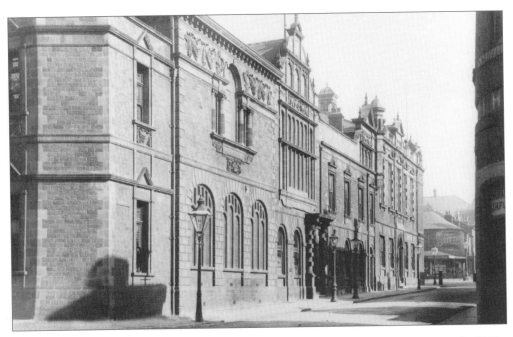

Howard Street, *c.* 1910. The borough council remodelled the town hall block on Howard Street in the 1890s. Nearest the camera is the borough magistrates' courts, followed by the town hall with the Assembly Rooms on the corner of Effingham Street. In the distance is Brittain's shop on the corner of Henry Street. (*Rotherham Archives & Local Studies 2772*)

Howard Street, July 2001. When the borough council moved out of the town hall complex in 1988 it was converted into the Old Town Hall shopping arcade. Burger King has replaced the Courts. (*Author*)

ral Library, Howard Street, 1931. The town's original library, on Market Street, was gutted by fire in 1925. The library
ved to temporary accommodation in a wooden hut on Corporation Street until the new Central Library was ready in 1931.
herham Archives & Local Studies 6723)

ard Street, July
1. The library moved
e new Central
ry and Arts Centre
/alker Place in 1976.
Amber Centre stands
e site of the 1931
ing. (*Author*)

The lending library, Howard Street, 1931. This shows the new lending library, with its oak fittings, shortly before it opened to the public. (*Rotherham Archives & Local Studies 6731*)

The lending library, Walker Place, July 2001. (*Author*)

The Regent Theatre, Howard Street, October 1957. The theatre opened in 1895 as the Theatre Royal. Converted into a cinema in 1915, it was renamed the Regent in 1930 when sound was installed. It was converted back into a theatre in 1935 and survived until 1957. At the upper left is the rear of the Hippodrome on Henry Street. (*Rotherham Archives & Local Studies 872*)

Howard Street, July 2001. These shops on Howard Street were built as part of the new Centenary Market development, opened in 1971. (*Author*)

Court no. 1, Howard Street, February 1930. These slum houses were at the Doncaster Road end of Howard Street, in the section formerly known as Pigeon Lane. Harry Seddon's wireless store can just be seen at the left. The houses were demolished soon after the photograph was taken. (*Rotherham Archives & Local Studies 2635*)

Howard Street, July 2001. The Doncaster Supply Stores were erected on the site of Court no. 1 in 1938. The building later became part of Brittain's new store and is now occupied by Riley's snooker hall. Seddon's store was replaced by the 1960 extension to Rotherham College of Arts and Technology. (*Author*)

Wellgate
& Westgate

Wellgate from the bottom of High Street, July 2001. (*Author*)

Wellgate from the bottom of High Street, *c.* 1905. The new bank is at the right. At the left is part of the Pack Horse Inn (closed 1904) with Richard Watson Cox & Co., drapers, at nos 1 and 3 Wellgate. (*Rotherham Archives & Local Studies 00176*)

Nos 9–15 Wellgate, *c.* 1890. Charles Harvey, music seller and concert agent, occupied no. 9 with the Rotherham Conservative Club on the upper floors. Albert Varah, grocer, was at no. 11, no. 13 was derelict and John Bottomley, shoemaker, was at no. 15. (*Rotherham Archives & Local Studies 00189*)

Nos 9–15 Wellgate, July 2001. All the buildings in the earlier photograph have gone, replaced by Lloyds TSB Bank (nos 9–11) and Wilbefort, clothiers (nos 13–15). (*Author*)

gate, looking north, *c.* 1906. Horse-drawn transport is well in evidence with a line of delivery carts drawn up outside the Coach, which is undergoing refurbishment (left). Two doors to the right, the lower building was the original Cleaver. *herham Archives & Local Studies 11553)*

gate, looking north, 2001. Denham's ing is largely anged but the ver (for a time known Ginty's, now the nd Shive) was lt in 1926. (*Author*)

The Mail Coach Inn, Wellgate, *c.* 1910. William G. Foster was the landlord from 1908 to 1916. The brewers Whitworth, Son & Nephew were based at Wath upon Dearne. (*Rotherham Archives & Local Studies 14752*)

The Mail Coach Inn, Wellgate, July 2001. Now a John Smith's pub, the Mail Coach no longer displays its elaborate rooftop sign. (*Author*)

No. 24 Wellgate, *c.* 1912. Miss E. Gregory's corset shop at 24 Wellgate had formerly housed Pontis's medical botanist business. (*Rotherham Archives & Local Studies 15889*)

No. 24 Wellgate, July 2001. Still in the female clothing trade, no. 24 is now home to the Ks boutique. (*Author*)

Nos 42–44 Wellgate, 1939. The small car with the L-plate is parked outside Ernest Sayers, insurance broker, at 42 Well
Mr Sayers was also co-proprietor of the Rotherham School of Motoring. No. 44 was the Oddfellows Inn, closed in 1938
prominent sign for Bentley's Beer is on the side of the Hare and Hounds. (*Rotherham Archives & Local Studies 0187*)

Nos 42–44 Wellgate, J
2001. Only the Hare &
Hounds remains today,
Sayers and the Oddfell
having gone to make u
for a car park. (*Author*

ate, 1939. Placards advertising saloon car trips to Blackpool stand outside Wilfred Stansfield's confectioner's shop. th the Swan Vestas sign is the narrow entry to Court no. 8, Wellgate. To the right of Ernest Giles, optician, is a private occupied by Joseph Leslie Whitehead, colliery surfaceman. (*Rotherham Archives & Local Studies 0184*)

ate, July 2001. The ate multi-storey car now stands on the site shops in the earlier graph. (*Author*)

No. 69 Wellgate, *c.* 190
Joseph Crooks's greengr
shop stood on the corne
with Wellgate Mount. N
the bananas hanging in
doorway and the advert
'English grapes' (presum
hothouse grown) and 'E
wallnuts'. (*Rotherham
Archives & Local Studies
0177*)

Nos 67–69 Wellgate, Ju
2001. After some years
an estate agent's, nos 6
69 now house the *Rothe
Advertiser* and *Rotherha*
Record shop. (*Author*)

Wellgate, looking south, *c.* 1906. A large load of hay makes its way out of town in the distance. F. Bingham's cash chemist's shop stood on the corner with Sherwood Crescent, with Maurice Creswick, draper, on the near corner. (*Rotherham Archives & Local Studies 11608*)

Wellgate, looking south, July 2001. The buildings have changed little, although a private detective now occupies the top floor of Bingham's former shop. (*Author*)

Wellgate, looking north, *c.* 1925. This view from the junction of Wellgate and Hollowgate shows the Three Tuns (closed 1938) at the left. In the distance the tower with the dome on top marks the Primitive Methodist Chapel. The tram tracks are still visible in the centre of the road but the overhead wiring has been altered for trolley-buses. (*Rotherham Archives & Local Studies 1613*)

Wellgate, looking north, July 2001. The Three Tuns disappeared as part of a slum clearance campaign. Immediately beyond the Three Tuns was the Central Motor Works. This developed into Henly's motor showroom, now Perry's. (*Author*)

M. Wilde's general store, 169 Wellgate, 1972. The arrow indicates an oil lamp bracket, a survival of Rotherham's early nineteenth-century street lighting. (*Rotherham Archives & Local Studies 0173*)

No. 169 Wellgate, July 2001. The lamp bracket has gone and Wilde's is now the Bombay Curry House. (*Author*)

Court no. 13, Wellgate, 1933. The pavement along the left-hand side of Court no. 13 was part of a narrow walkway known as Spinners Walk, connecting Wellgate with Hollowgate. The Esso globe at the left marks the edge of Moorhouse & Co.'s garage and taxi premises. (*Rotherham Archives & Local Studies 0191*)

Jet petrol station, Wellgate, July 2001. Court no. 13 was demolished in the early 1930s. Spinners Walk still exists, running between the petrol station and Kwik Save to Warwick Street. (*Author*)

Wellgate House, Wellgate, 1965. Wellgate House had fallen on hard times when this photograph was taken. In the mid-nineteenth century it was the home of John Aldred, proprietor of a successful chemical works on Wellgate. Charles Green, builder, who used the elegant gardens as his builder's yard, bought it in 1889. In about 1910 another builder, H. Treherne, converted the house into three dwellings and between the wars the yard was used by Moorhouse & Co.'s garage and taxi business. (*Rotherham Archives & Local Studies 0196*)

Kwik Save, Wellgate, July 2001. The supermarket occupies the site of Wellgate House. (*Author*)

H.S. Bristowe's delivery van outside the 'Shop at the Corner', at the junction of Wellgate and Gerard Road, 1939. Note how the tram tracks disappear under the tarmac near the junction with Aldred Street. (*Rotherham Archives & Local Studies 0185*)

Wellgate, July 2001. The tram tracks and trolley-bus wires are long gone but the 'Shop at the Corner' is still there, now known as Wellgate Stores and liberally advertising 'Irn-Bru'. (*Author*)

lgate School, *c.* 1900. Wellgate School, at the corner of Wellgate and Aldred Street, was erected by the Rotherham School
rd in 1879. (*Rotherham Archives & Local Studies 3503*)

of Wellgate School,
2001. The school
d in 1963 and the
ling was put to a
ber of uses before
olition in 1993.
sing now occupies
ite. (*Author*)

The Ship Hotel, Westgate, c. 1890. The hotel was so called because it stood on the corner with Ship Hill, which derived its na from a corruption of 'Sheep Hill', being the road connecting the High Street and Westgate with the beast market in the Cr (*Rotherham Archives & Local Studies 14227*)

Mazeppa Chambers, Westgate, Ju 2001. This block was erected in 1 following the closure of the Ship 1933. Originally incorporating a dance hall, the block now contai the M@zeppa Bar, the Revolution nightclub and a solicitor's. (*Auth*

Westgate, looking north, *c.* 1932. A trolley-bus is just turning the corner from Westgate into Main Street on a damp day in the early 1930s. The lorry is passing the Station Hotel and E.J. Brown & Co.'s ironmonger's shop. The Station Hotel was so called because it stood opposite the Westgate terminus of the Sheffield & Rotherham Railway. (*Rotherham Archives & Local Studies 0164*)

Westgate, looking north, July 2001. The Station Hotel and the adjoining block (now Akhtar's Martial Arts Academy) were rebuilt in 1935. After several changes of name the Station is now the Millennium. (*Author*)

Labour exchange, Westgate, *c.* 1912. This building was originally constructed as the terminus building at Westgate station on the Sheffield to Rotherham line, opened in 1838. When it was replaced with a simpler station building on Main Street, the old terminus was converted into offices. It served as the main post office from 1880 until 1907 and became the labour exchange in 1910. It fulfilled this function until the new labour exchange on Moorgate Street opened in 1938. (*Rotherham Archives & Local Studies 0119*)

Post office sorting depot, Westgate, July 2001. In later years the old station building reverted to railway use as a control centre. It was demolished in the 1960s and the sorting office now stands on the site. (*Author*)

Westgate, 1933. This block of shops on Westgate disappeared during the slum clearances in 1933–4. From right to left: Walter Montgomery, hairdresser; William Douglas, shopkeeper; Alfred Percy Telling's Westgate Meat Store; and John Williams, shopkeeper. Between Telling's and Williams's shops is the narrow entry to Court no. 8, Westgate. At the left is one of the gateposts of the Westgate Mission Room. (*Rotherham Archives & Local Studies 0114*)

Westgate, July 2001. The telephone exchange was erected on the site of Court no. 8 in 1939 and has since been considerably extended. (*Author*)

Westgate Green, *c.* 1905. This was in the early days of Rotherham Corporation Tramways, before the trams were fitted w top covers. The tram in the centre is en route to the Canklow terminus, with another tram on the line to Tinsley just visible the left. Between the two is the Traveller's Rest with the White Swan just visible to its right. (*Rotherham Archives & Local Stud 0152*)

Westgate Green, 2001. The Traveller's closed in 1909 and was replaced by premises for J. Clayton, motor engineers. The W Swan was rebuilt in 1922 and is still in business. (*Author*)

The Dusty Miller, Westgate, *c.* 1893. E. Parkinson was landlord from 1885 to 1893. The pub derived its name from its proximity to Robinson's corn mill. (*Rotherham Archives & Local Studies 0132*)

The Dusty Miller, Canklow Road, 1984. The pub was rebuilt in 1894. The southern end of Westgate, between Alma Road and Sheffield Road, was renumbered as part of Canklow Road in 1936. (*Rotherham Archives & Local Studies 0136*)

The Baths foundry, Westgate, *c.* 1890. This was one of several foundries off Westgate and took its name from the ea nineteenth-century public baths on the banks of the Don. (*Rotherham Archives & Local Studies 0129*)

The site of the Bath Foundry, 2001. Th BT telephone excha can be seen in the distance. (*Author*)

Effingham Street & Frederick Street

Effingham Street, July 2001. Two of the Effingham Street shops, Lipton's store, now Phones 4U, and Fletcher's, now the PDSA shop, survive from the following photograph. (*Author*)

Effingham Street, *c.* 1905. Effingham Street was constructed in the early 1850s as a part of a development carried out by the Earl of Effingham, lord of the manor of Rotherham. In the early days of the tramway system, tram no. 1 waits outside Lipton's grocer's shop, with the Stove Grate Workers' Union offices above. To the right is W.R. Fletcher, butcher. (*Rotherham Archives & Local Studies 17912*)

College Square, Effingham Street, *c.* 1910. On the east side of Effingham Street stood the Court House, constructed in 1826 to replace the eighteenth-century town hall. Sheffield tram no. 86 waits to return to the city on the joint Rotherham/Sheffield service. Behind the tram is St George's Hall and beyond that the Zion Methodist Chapel at the junction of Effingham Street and Henry Street. (*Rotherham Archives & Local Studies 3872*)

Effingham Street, July 2001. The last tram ran in 1949. The Court House closed in 1929 and Woolworth's redeveloped the site in 1930. (*Author*)

:tion of Effingham Street and Howard Street, *c.* 1972. C&A's store replaced the Hippodrome which closed in 1959. Beyond
A's is the entrance to the Centenary Market, opened in 1971. The fountain outside C&A's had an unfortunate habit of
nching passers-by. (*Rotherham Archives & Local Studies 17967*)

:tion of Effingham
et and Howard Street,
2001. The original
tain was replaced
more conventional,
level fountains.
's store is now a
ch of the Halifax.
hor)

The Effingham Arms, at the junction of Effingham Street and Frederick Street, 1891. The Effingham Arms dates from 1860. It is seen here in June 1891, decorated for the visit of the Prince of Wales (later Edward VII) to open Clifton Park. (*Rotherham Archives & Local Studies 5099*)

The Effingham Arms, July 2001. The structure of the Effingham Arms remains intact. The ground floor was clad in polished granite in the 1930s but this has recently been covered with wooden panelling. (*Author*)

Effingham Square, 1913. Actually a triangle, Effingham Square was formed by the intersection of Frederick Street, Effingham Street and Drummond Street. The Hastings Clock in the centre was a gift to the town by local businessman James Hastings to mark George V's coronation in 1912. Behind the clock is George Bingham's grocer's shop on the corner of Frederick Street and Drummond Street. (*Rotherham Archives & Local Studies 4519*)

Effingham Square, July 2001. The Hastings Clock was re-erected next to the Civic Building in 1969, having been in store since the square was converted into a roundabout in 1961. The roundabout gave way to the present flowerbeds in 1996, as part of the pedestrianisation of Effingham Street and Frederick Street. (*Author*)

No. 20 Frederick Street, *c.* 1905. Typical of many small stores in the town, Sarah Morte's grocer's shop stood next to the Effingham House pub. (*Rotherham Archives & Local Studies 0874*)

(*Below*): Frederick Street, July 2001. This stretch of Frederick Street was redeveloped as the Ceres Building in 1961. (*Author*)

Reindeer Inn, 1907. This inn stood at the junction of Nottingham Street and Frederick Street, and was badly damaged by a explosion in February 1907. Eastwood Methodist Chapel is visible in the background. (*Rotherham Archives & Local Studies 89*)

site of the Reindeer
July 2001. Nothing
grass now marks
ite of the Reindeer,
h closed in 1967.
hor)

Tusmore Street, *c.* 1910. One of T.W. Outram's hearses pictured outside his premises at 35 Tusmore Street. This appears to be a dual-purpose vehicle, with accommodation for the coffin and the mourners. (*Rotherham Archives & Local Studies 15656*)

The site of Outram's premises in Tusmore Street, July 2001. Today only a clump of trees outside Norfolk House marks the site. (*Author*)

The Howard Hotel, 1966. This area of Rotherham was well supplied with public houses. The Howard Hotel stood at the junction of Tusmore Street, Kenneth Street and Effingham Street. This photograph was taken in the year the pub closed. (*Rotherham Archives & Local Studies 3198*)

Effingham Street, July 2001. The property on Tusmore and Kenneth Streets was demolished to make way for the council offices on Walker Place and the inner ring road. The St Ann's Medical Centre now stands on the site of the Howard Hotel. (*Author*)

Frederick Street from St Ann's Road, 1965. Plowman's chemist's shop is at the right with Wiley & Co., wine and spirit merchants, at the left. Part of the Salvation Army Citadel (formerly the National School) on Kenneth Street can be seen over the wall behind Plowman's. (*Rotherham Archives & Local Studies 2916*)

St Ann's roundabout, July 2001. The site of Plowman's shop now lies in the centre of the roundabout at the junction of Centenary Way and St Ann's Road. (*Author*)

The view from St Ann's Flats, July 1967. Most of the houses between Drummond Street and St Ann's Road were demolished in the late 1960s. This was partly to make way for Centenary Way and partly to clear the sites for the building of new council offices. Effingham Square can be seen in the distance with the bus station at the right. Tusmore Street runs across the foreground. (*Rotherham Archives & Local Studies 6868*)

Centenary Way, July 2001. The same view today, with Centenary Way in the foreground. The Civic Buildings can be seen to the left with Crinoline House at the right. (*Author*)

Fitzwilliam Road from Frederick Street, *c.* 1904. The original Eastwood Methodist Chapel stands at the west end of Fitzwilliam Road, with the Sunday School beyond it. The original postcard identifies the two children marked with crosses as Miss Bell and Master Bell. In the background, Fitzwilliam Road is still largely undeveloped. (*Rotherham Archives & Local Studies* 15853)

Fitzwilliam Road, July 2001. The Sunday School still exists but the chapel was rebuilt in the 1960s. (*Author*)

Moorgate Street & Moorgate Road

Downs Row, Moorgate Street, July 2001. Downs Row leads from Moorgate Street to the top of Oil Mill Fold. It is now lined by offices, with the former Unitarian Chapel, also now offices, in the distance. (*Author*)

Downs Row, Moorgate Street, 1933. Some of the inhabitants of Downs Row posed for the borough council's photographer when he was gathering evidence to support the demolition of the slum housing. At the far end is the Unitarian Chapel, founded in 1704 and rebuilt in 1842. (*Rotherham Archives & Local Studies 4731*)

Rotherham Grammar School, Moorgate Road, 1880. In 1857 the Feoffees of the Common Lands erected this building on Moorgate for the Grammar School. The master's house was on the right with the schoolroom on the left. (*Rotherham Archives & Local Studies 8096*)

The former Rotherham Grammar School, Moorgate Road, July 2001. The clock tower and the turret over the master's front door may have gone, but the building is still much the same as when the school moved out in 1890. (*Author*)

South Grove, Moorgate Road, 1907. The house known as South Grove was erected in the eighteenth century by corn merchant Thomas Wheatcroft. In 1901 it became a centre for the training of pupil teachers. (*Rotherham Archives & Local Studies 15884*)

South Grove School, Moorgate Road, July 2001. The original house was replaced by a new secondary school in 1911. South Grove Comprehensive School closed in 1987. Part of the building is now used by the borough council's training section. (*Author*)

Rotherstoke, Moorgate Road, *c.* 1925. This was one of a number of large houses built on Moorgate by industrialists in nineteenth century. Rotherstoke was the home of George Haywood, a partner in Yates & Haywood, stove grate makers. I twentieth century the house became an old people's home. (*Rotherham Archives & Local Studies 10985*)

Rotherstoke Close, Moorgat July 2001. With demolition Rotherstoke in 1978, the si was used for low-rise apartm (*Author*)

...erham Grammar School, Moorgate Road, *c.* 1930. Erected in 1876 as a college for training Independent ministers, ...imposing building was vacated in 1888 and purchased by the Feoffees as new accommodation for the grammar school. ...*herham Archives & Local Studies 8952)*

...as Rotherham College, July 2001. With the introduction of comprehensive education to Rotherham in 1967, the ...mar School became Thomas Rotherham Sixth Form College. (*Author*)

Moorgate Cemetery, Boston Castle Grove, *c.* 1890. The cemetery began as a private enterprise in 1841 and was sol
the Rotherham Burial Board in 1855 for £2,500. When the churchyard was closed in 1854, Moorgate Cemetery bec
the main burial ground for the town. (*Rotherham Archives & Local Studies 0997*)

Moorgate Cemetery, Boston Castle Grove, July 2001. There have been few burials at Moorgate since the new cemetery a
Herringthorpe opened in 1953. Ivy and other foliage is slowly swallowing many of the Victorian monuments. (*Author*)

Boston Park, *c.* 1910. In 1876 the corporation leased Boston Castle and the surrounding land from the Earl of Effingham to form Boston Park, the town's first public park. It was originally known as Rotherham Park or the People's Park. Among the attractions was this relocated doorway from the medieval College of Jesus in the town centre. (*Rotherham Archives & Local Studies 2191*)

Boston Park, July 2001. The Jesus College doorway today. (*Author*)

The bowling green, Boston Park, *c.* 1900. In 1876 a bowling green was provided in Boston Park, served by this stone pavilion. Behind the pavilion, a set of steps climbs the rock face to the upper level of the park. (*Rotherham Archives & Local Studies 0776*)

The bowling green, Boston Park, July 2001. There is still bowling in Boston Park. The steel container is a temporary bowling pavilion, replacing the wooden one that was destroyed by arson at New Year 2001. (*Author*)

Doncaster Gate & Doncaster Road

Doncaster Gate, *c.* 1896. The Wheatsheaf can be seen in the centre of the photograph. The three-storey building at the right was occupied by Thomas J. Campsall, veterinary surgeon. (*Rotherham Archives & Local Studies 16395*)

Doncaster Gate, *c.* 1919. This later view down Doncaster Gate shows the Moorish domes and tile cladding of the Cinema House, opened in March 1914. At the right can be seen the rebuilt Wheatsheaf of 1909–10, on the corner of Howard Street. (*Rotherham Archives & Local Studies 2598*)

Doncaster Gate, July 2001. The exuberant exterior of the Cinema House was removed in the 1960s in favour of a very nondescript replacement. The cinema closed in 1964 but the building reopened immediately as a bingo hall. (*Author*)

Clifton Park, *c.* 1920. After the First World War the government presented the town with this war surplus Mark IV tank. It stood on the base of the Victorian bandstand which had been moved to Ferham Park before the war. (*Rotherham Archives & Local Studies 14209*)

Clifton Park, July 2001. The tank was removed in 1927 and the present bandstand erected on the site. The bandstand was refurbished for Queen Elizabeth II's visit to mark the centenary of the park in 1991. (*Author*)

Clifton Park, 1910. Birdcage Lodge on Doncaster Road was one of the original lodges to the Clifton House estate. By 1910 it was guarding one of the entrances into Clifton Park. (*Rotherham Archives & Local Studies 10276*)

Clifton Park, July 2001. Flowerbeds now mark the site of Birdcage Lodge. (*Author*)

The Eastwood Inn, Doncaster Road, *c.* 1910. A fishing party waits to set off in the years before the First World War. The charabanc is a Sheffield-built Durham Churchill. (*Rotherham Archives & Local Studies 3814*)

The Eastwood Inn, Doncaster Road, July 2001. This is the modern Eastwood Inn after extensions in the 1930s to cope with the increased business following the building of the East Dene housing estate in the 1920s. (*Author*)

Nos 383–385 Doncaster Road, 1953. The shop is decorated to celebrate the coronation of Queen Elizabeth II. (*Rotherham Archives & Local Studies 3805*)

Nos 383–385 Doncaster Road, July 2001. It is still a general store, but is now known as Gilbert's Stop and Shop. (*Author*)

The pumping station, at the junction of Doncaster Road and Fitzwilliam Road, 1905. A tram stands at the pumping station terminus. The pumping station was erected in 1887 to pump water from Dalton Brook and Aldwarke Spring for the town water supply. (*Rotherham Archives & Local Studies 16836*)

The pumping station site, July 2001. Today only the pumping station house, now a fish and chip shop, remains behind the trees beyond the roundabout. In the distance can be seen the Mushroom Garage at the top of Herringthorpe Valley Road. (*Author*)

No. 531 Fitzwilliam Road, c. 1935. Lucy Tummy ran t shop at the corner of Fitzwil Road and Watkin Street fro 1916 to 1939. (*Rotherham Archives & Local Studies 486*

Springwell Gardens, Fitzwilli Road, July 2001. The shop was demolished as part of th development of Oakhill Flats 1970–1. Most of the flats we recently demolished and repl with an estate of semi-detac houses known as Springwell Gardens. (*Author*)

Masbrough &
Kimberworth

Chapel on the Bridge from Masbrough, *c.* 1910. Both the bridge and the chapel date from the 1480s. The chapel had a chequered life after it was suppressed (as a chantry chapel) in 1547. Initially used as almshouses, it became the town jail in 1778 and it is seen here in use as a tobacconist's shop. (*Rotherham Archives & Local Studies 1462*)

Chapel on the Bridge from Masbrough, *c.* 1913. A closer view of the chapel, showing the small windows inserted in the original gothic openings. The tobacconist was bought out in 1913 with a view to restoring the building as a place of worship. But the war intervened and it was not until 1924 that the chapel was restored and reconsecrated. (*Rotherham Archives & Local Studies 15871*)

Chapel on the Bridge, July 2001. In 1930, when the new Chantry Bridge was constructed alongside, the medieval bridge was reduced to its original dimensions. (*Author*)

...ough, 1970. This view ...brough was presumably ...from one of the cranes ...ng the multi-storey car ...bove the bus station. ...try ramp over the Don ...under construction. ...undabout on the far ...was the temporary end ...first section of the inner ...oad, Centenary Way. ...e far bank, the property ...asbrough Street awaits ...ition to make way for ...ntenary Way extension ...v Bridge. (*Rotherham ...es & Local Studies 7012*)

...rough, July 2001. A modern view from the top of the car park shows Centenary Way replacing the roundabout in the ...ous view. The two-toned building to the left of the trees in the centre of the picture can be seen at the extreme right of the ...view. This was, until 1998, part of the Bestobell Valves factory. (*Author*)

Masbrough Street, *c.* 1910. The premises of William Middleton, tailor, clothier and hatter, is prominent in this row of s
extending from Orchard Street to Queens Road. Next door was Kendrick Fieldsend, pawnbroker. (*Rotherham Archives &*
Studies 3778)

Masbrough Street, July 2
The property between Or
Street and Queen Street fe
of the clearances to make
for Centenary Way.

. 151 Masbrough Street, 1932. Emma Fowler was viously proud that her off-licence was not tied to y particular brewery. Among the beers stocked were ntley's, Gilmour's, Inde Coope's, Whitbread's and ux. (*Rotherham Archives & Local Studies 14652*)

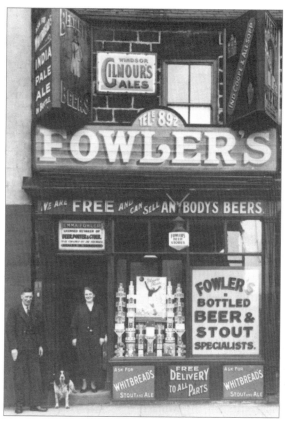

No. 151 Masbrough Street, July 2001. Fowler's shop is now the Planet Pizza & Burger Bar. (*Author*)

117

Bray's Building, Masbrough Street, *c.* 1905. Henry Bray's elaborate general store stood at the corner of Masbrough Street and Victoria Street in the early years of the twentieth century. The left-hand portion was converted into the Tivoli Cinema in 1913, giving its name to the Tivoli End of Rotherham United's ground across the road. (*Rotherham Archives & Local Studies 2793*)

Car park, Masbrough Street, July 2001. The Tivoli closed in 1959 and became a furniture store. This was demolished in 1988 and the site is now used as a car park by Rotherham United FC. (*Author*)

Kimberworth Road, Kimberworth, *c.* 1905. This shows the Kimberworth tram terminus, with a tram waiting to return to Rotherham. The horse-drawn vehicle is the tramways tower wagon, used to maintain the overhead wires. Behind the tram stands the original Kimberworth Wesleyan Chapel of 1827 and the new chapel of 1904. (*Rotherham Archives & Local Studies* 5346)

Kimberworth Road, Kimberworth, July 2001. The 1904 chapel is now used as a dance and fitness studio. The 1827 chapel has given way to housing. (*Author*)

St Thomas's Church, Kimberworth, from Meadowhall Road, *c.* 1915. Kimberworth was part of the parish of Rotherham and did not get its own church until 1843, becoming a separate parish in 1849. (*Rotherham Archives & Local Studies 5352*)

St Thomas's Church, Kimberworth, from Meadowhall Road, July 2001. The cottages in front of the church, on Peter Street, still exist but are now shrouded by trees. (*Author*)

Suburbia

Whiston crossroads, *c.* 1905. This horse and cart, with spare horse behind, is standing in West Bawtry Road, near the turn to Moorgate Road. (*Rotherham Archives & Local Studies 050*)

Whiston crossroads, *c.* 1935. The same crossroads just before work started on widening the former Castle Sike Lane (now East Bawtry Road) up to the Brecks. Suburban development has already started on the new building line. (*Rotherham Archives & Local Studies 049*)

Whiston crossroads, July 2001. The former sleepy intersection is now a busy lights-controlled crossing. (*Author*)

Nos 487–491 Herringthorpe Valley Road, 1937. Herringthorpe Valley Road was constructed in 1933 to link the main road to Doncaster to the road to Maltby. The bungalow, no. 487, Chalford, was built for Joe Akroyd, a partner in the Rotherham architects J.E. Knight & Co., to his own design, in 1934. The houses were within Whiston parish until the borough boundary was extended in 1936. (*Rotherham Archives & Local Studies 8682*)

Nos 487–491 Herringthorpe Valley Road, July 2001. The houses are little changed today, although the trees are considerably larger. (*Author*)

Brunswick Road, Broom Valley, 1973. The Broom Valley council housing estate was started in 1950. At the bottom of the hill can be seen St Barnabas' Church, opened in 1951 as a dual-purpose church and community centre. (*Rotherham Archives & Local Studies 1263*)

Brunswick Road, Broom Valley, July 2001.

Acknowledgements

All the 'Past' photographs in this book are chosen from the Illustrations Collection of the Archives & Local Studies Section of Rotherham Central Library. This collection of some 20,000 images chronicles the changing face of Rotherham from the 1860s to the present day. Thanks are due to the many members of the public who have donated originals or copies of photographs to the collection. Particular thanks are due to Mr R. Cogill for permission to reproduce the 'Past' photographs on pages 48, 69, 71, 91 and 92.

The 'Present' photographs were taken by the author during July 2001. For the technically minded they were taken on a Canon Eos 300 camera with a Canon 35–85 lens on a mixture of Kodak and Ilford film.

Particular thanks are due to the staff of the Archives & Local Studies Section (Marcia, Pat and Sally), to Sarah Crossland for access to the parish church tower and to Linda for proof reading and keeping the coffee flowing.